Lost Dreams

Further titles in this series

A Busker on Bow Street

The Farmer's Son

The Seasonal Visitor

Lost Dreams

Short Stories for Adult Learners No. 2

LinguaBooks Readers

Copyright © 2018 LinguaBooks

The right of the individual authors to be identified as the authors of the stories included in this collection has been asserted in accordance with sections 77 and 78 of the Copyright, Designs and Patents Act 1988.

Published in the United Kingdom by LinguaBooks

ISBN: 978-1-911369-11-0

A CIP catalogue record for this book is available from the British Library.

Series editor: Maurice Claypole
Edited by: Ann Claypole
Proofreader: Marie-Christin Strobel

Every effort has been made to trace the holders of intellectual property rights in respect of the content of this publication but the publishers will be pleased to hear from any copyright holder whom we have been unable to contact. If notified, the publisher will attempt to rectify any errors or omissions at the earliest opportunity.

LinguaBooks
Elsie Whiteley Innovation Centre
Hopwood Lane, Halifax HX1 5ER
www.linguabooks.com

After nourishment, shelter and companionship, stories are the thing we need most in the world.

– Philip Pullman

ACKNOWLEDGEMENTS

Some of these stories first appeared in *The Written Word*, a journal for English-speaking residents of Baden-Württemberg, Germany.

The publishers would like to thank the authors of the original stories for offering their work for publication and similarly to express their gratitude to all who were involved in producing both *The Written Word* and the present collection, thereby enabling these stories to reach a wider audience within the context of adult literacy and language learning.

Image credits: cover, page 9, 22, 33, 42, 53 Dreamstime; 21, 41, 65 pixabay; 32 kisspng.com, aeromd.com, Mobi Supply, LLC; 52 colourbox.com

Contents

Introduction

This LinguaBooks Reader is the second volume of short stories to be published in this innovative new series.

The stories are presented as originally written by native speakers of English from a variety of countries and backgrounds. Although the punctuation and spelling have largely been harmonised, no attempt has been made to simplify or sanitise the language used. The main objective here is to give learners and other readers an authentic language experience whilst at the same time providing plenty of scope for language acquisition, enhanced awareness and vocabulary expansion. From a point of view of difficulty, the language varies in terms of complexity and register and may be considered equivalent to Level C1 of the Common European Framework of Reference for Languages (CEFR).

The content and scope make each book in this series ideal for classroom use, but the stories can also be read for pleasure, with or without recourse to the supplementary material included. The words and phrases explained after each story provide useful assistance, but lay no claim to completeness, since learners nowadays have ready access to a wide range of external resources. Autonomous learners who favour an active approach will also benefit from the activities and puzzles, which represent a combination of consolidation and discovery exercises. An answer key is provided for the convenience of learners, teachers and independent readers.

Lost Dreams

by Deirdre Mclaughlin

— ❧ ❧ —

The sky over Winchester was overcast and the first drops of rain landed on her shoulders as she pressed her palm against the brass push plate on the door of the Red Lion.

She hadn't been in for ages. It may seem weird to long for the musty, beery tang that often hangs in the air of a public house, but this had been 'her' pub. She loved to be among friends, to chat about people, business, politics or just ordinary everyday life. She had found lots of friends there, people she would talk to once or twice and who then vanished for a couple of months only to return with renewed energy, more experience, new ideas. She, on the other hand, seemed to derive all her strength, her energy and experience from this place and its people. She used to love just sitting and listening to folk talking about their interests and their way of life. She saw this as her path to wisdom. People were always very kind, taking her into their confidence, buying her drinks or just passing the time of day. She knew nearly everyone, either by sight or as an acquaintance. She had her friends among the bartenders, the staff and the regulars. In short, it was her dream come true being a part of this big 'family'.

She spent a lot of time just hanging out in this special place and it was little wonder that her other interests suffered as a result. So much so that she had to give herself a break. So, one evening in late summer, she parted from her friends and what had become her second home.

At first, the separation made her feel a bit strange. Then she felt a kind of chill going through all her friendships. Over the next three months, things didn't turn out as well as she had hoped; people didn't call her as much as they had promised, and she got the feeling that something was going wrong, something had changed. She longed to go back; She suffered horribly under the strain of being away.

This grey November evening was her first opportunity to return. She went down to the pub at her old time, at about six in the evening. She had arranged to meet one of her girlfriends at half past six. She saw the change immediately: the green-painted door, once well-polished and spotless, was dirty, with the paint peeling off. At the bottom of the stairs there was a swing door with a window in the upper half – one of those covered with colourful flowers and ornaments. She was shocked: the door was sagging on its hinges and the window was so grimy that she could hardly see inside. Suddenly she stopped. What on earth was wrong? She listened hard: Nothing! Where were all the happy voices she used to hear when she came down the steps, the soft murmuring and clattering that drifted up the stairs to the street? Now all was silent: no voices, no chinking of glasses, only a faint humming of a far-away singer emanating from the speakers of a sound system.

She looked through the window into a gloomy room, empty, unfamiliar, grey. She was taken aback. What had happened? Was it because it had turned to winter, or had things really changed in such a short time? She walked in; no voices greeted her. She looked around: The bar, once so familiar, bright, crowded and vibrant, was now dirty, nearly deserted. The tables and chairs, once so neatly arranged, now stood around in complete disorder.

A voice asked her what she would like to drink. She ordered her usual tipple from a totally unfamiliar barman and sat down to wait.

The ringing of a phone in the distance broke the silence. The barman hurried excitedly towards the sound as if it might save him from dying of boredom. As he stood with his eyes turned towards the entrance she could see his face clearly. It brightened up when he put the receiver to his ear, as if he were used to changing his expression when talking to a customer. But that look vanished quickly as he told the caller to wait a second. He called out her name. Surprised, she left her stool and went over to the phone. It was her friend, who was full of apologies but had to work late and would not be there for another hour or so.

She pulled out her mobile phone: no signal, not even a bar or a blip; that's why the call had come in on the landline. She couldn't even log on to social networks. What was she supposed to do for another hour if no one came in? In despair, she ordered another drink. What now? No one to talk to, nothing interesting going on. In the mirror opposite she could see the stairs and the door. At least she could see who was coming down.

With no conversation and not even a newspaper in sight, her attention turned to offline games. After what seemed like an eternity, she had crashed out on Candy Crush, got totally tired of Tetris and had her fill of Funny Furries when she heard footsteps descending.

A glance in the mirror told her that this was definitely not her friend. So, she snapped the wallet of her phone shut and was on the point of rising to leave when she heard the unmistakable clickety-click of high heels. Long legs appeared in the mirror followed by a miniskirt, an old pullover, an orange scarf, and a laughing face surrounded by a mop of red hair – a face which was more familiar to her than anything else since she had arrived. After a kiss on each cheek, they sat down, ordered drinks and exchanged the latest news and gossip.

She learned what had happened to the Red Lion. The owner had changed and many of the old bar staff and regulars had left. The new owner had soon run out of money. Prices had increased and people had gone where they could get the same but cheaper. Some of her friends still met up there occasionally. But many of them had left; they had got better jobs, moved away, vanished forever. What remained was now a small, unhappy crowd.

She sat there disheartened. How could all this have happened without her knowing? After a while, she decided to go away forever from this place, the place that had once been so dear to her. The dream was gone.

She put the blame on her friends for not telling her. It was worth rethinking the nature of those friendships again. She wasn't sure any more if those people had really been her friends.

A little while later, she and her friend left the Red Lion arm in arm, determined to find another place where they could relax and on her part, fired with a new desire to feel at home – and be part of a big, happy family once again.

— ◈ ◈ —

Words and phrases

overcast	cloudy
long for	want very strongly
tang	sharp smell or taste
derive	get
taken her into their confidence	trusted her with personal information or secrets
passing the time of day	chatting, making small talk
acquaintance	someone known to a person, but not a friend
sagging on its hinges	not hanging straight
grimy	dirty
murmuring	sound of low, indistinct voices
clattering	making a rattling sound
emanating	originating, being emitted
taken aback	shocked
vibrant	lively
her usual tipple	what she normally drank
supposed to	expected to, required to
glance	quick look
disheartened	discouraged, depressed
put the blame on her friends	held her friends responsible
rethinking	reconsidering
determined	resolved, with a firm intention

Food for thought

1. At the start of the story, how does she feel about the Red Lion?
   a. She is unsure what she will find when she enters.
   b. She knows that things will have changed.
   c. She has missed the atmosphere there.

2. Why did she decide to spend some time away from the pub?
   a. She found she was spending too much time there.
   b. She became tired of just hanging out.
   c. She didn't intend to stay away; it just happened.

3. Which word best describes the state of the pub when she enters?
   a. derelict
   b. neglected
   c. devastated

4. How did she spend her time while she was waiting for her friend?
   a. reading the newspaper
   b. making phone calls
   c. playing games

5. Which word best describes her state of mind at the end of the story?
   a. optimistic
   b. desperate
   c. depressed

Crossword puzzle

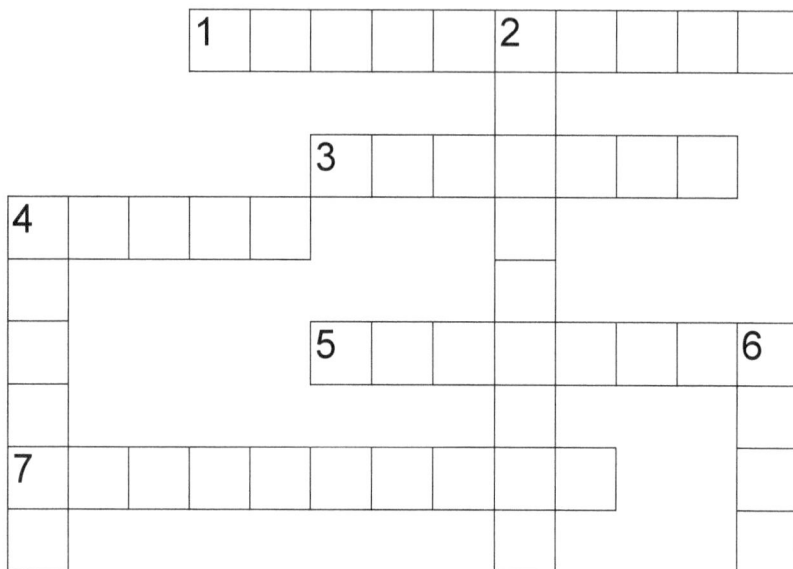

ACROSS
1 resolved
3 lively
4 dirty
5 cloudy
7 making a rattling sound

DOWN
2 sound of low voices
4 quick look
6 sharp smell or taste

Picture quiz – In a pub

A Here are some things you might find in a pub. Can you name them? Use the initial letters given.

1

2

3

4

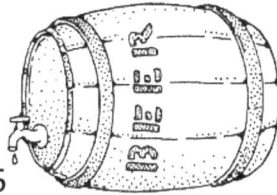
5

6

1 T_____ **2** D_____ **3** B_____S _____

4 I_____ B_____ **5** B_____ B _____ **6** B_____M _____

B In which of the pictures above can you see...

1 a tap ( ) **2** froth ( ) **3** double top ( )
4 a pedestal ( ) **5** a lid ( ) **6** a bottle ( )

Annie

by Anthony Curtis

— ❧ ❧ —

"Grandma!" called Annie softly.

There was no reply so little Annie tip-toed to the house to tell Mummy all about Grandma, who had chosen a very funny place to go to sleep.

She had expected some sort of reaction to her story, but she was totally unprepared for the commotion that followed. Mummy dropped a baking tray onto the floor, which made a terrible noise. Then, with a "Stay right where you are!" she rushed out into the garden, and little Annie, afraid that she had done something wrong, sat on a stool and pouted.

On the kitchen table stood a large plate of freshly baked currant buns. They smelled delicious. She only had to reach her hand out – but no, maybe she'd said something wrong – if she took one now, Mummy might be angry.

Three long minutes later, Mummy came into the kitchen and disappeared into the front room. Annie heard her voice, very loud and agitated.

"Yes, Doctor, I think it's her heart. My husband's at work and I'm not sure what to do."

The receiver was replaced and Mummy came back into the kitchen.

"Mummy," began Annie, wanting to ask about Grandma, but her mother said, "Don't bother me just now, Annie. You can have a bun if you want, but stay here and be quiet."

Annie slid off the stool and surveyed the buns. She wasn't sure which one to take so she recited, "Eeny, meeny, miny" pointing to each one in turn. Finally stopping at "moe", she decided that this particular bun was too small, so she looked for the one that had the most currants.

She was about to take the bun, but was interrupted by a wailing sound that came from the street. She knew what it was, of course. She'd seen one on the telly. It was an ambulance. The wailing was so loud Annie put her hands over her ears. When she removed them, the wailing had stopped. There was a slamming of doors. Annie grasped the kitchen stool and dragged it to the window. Wobbling precariously, she pulled back the lace curtains so that she had a clear view of the front garden. Yes, there was the ambulance, standing at the kerb opposite the front gate. A big red cross was painted on its side. Two large men in white were unloading something. It looked like a bed on wheels, and they pushed it over the front lawn (What will Mummy say?) and were soon out of sight. Annie clambered down from the stool and ran to the kitchen door. She could see her mother and the two men standing by the roses. Then the men lifted Grandma and put her on the bed on wheels. She was still asleep! Then they wheeled her away.

Annie didn't want to climb onto the stool again, it was too tiring, so she turned her attention once more to the buns. This time she took the first one that came. Munching loudly, she heard once more the slamming of doors, but the ambulance didn't wail when it drove off.

She was licking her fingers and contemplating the next bun when Mummy came into the kitchen, followed by the doctor. Mummy's eyes were red from weeping and the doctor looked very serious.

"I'll make a cup of tea," she said to the doctor.

"Thanks, but no," said the doctor." I'll be wanted elsewhere, most likely."

He came over to Annie and patted her gently on the head, but he didn't put his hand in his pocket for sweets as he usually did, so Annie climbed back on the stool and began to pout again. The doctor said goodbye, Mummy saw him out and then, as she came back and put the kettle on, Annie asked, "Mummy? Where's Grandma gone?"

She came to her daughter and pressed her to her bosom.

"Oh, my darling, Grandma's gone away. We'll never see her again."

"Never?"

With tears running down her cheeks, Mummy shook her head, and not knowing quite why, Annie felt like crying, too. Breaking from Mummy's embrace, she ran into the garden to the place where Grandma had lain. She saw the broken roses and suddenly she understood everything.

Grandma had gone to the same place where Joey had gone. Only a week ago, Joey had fallen off his perch and had lain quite still at the bottom of his cage. Mummy had taken him away, and in answer to Annie's questions had said that Joey had gone to heaven. Annie wasn't quite sure where heaven was, but it must be a very nice place. The next day, Mummy had come home with another Joey.

Fingering the roses, Annie thought, "If Grandma's gone to heaven, Mummy will bring me another one, but this time I shan't creep up behind her and say 'Booooooo!'"

— ❧ ❧ —

Words and phrases

tip-toed	walked quietly
commotion	fuss
baking tray	steel sheet used for making buns or biscuits, etc.
pouted	showed displeasure, sulked
currant	small, seedless raisin
agitated	upset, distressed, nervous
receiver	part of a telephone held to the ear
surveyed	inspected
eeny, meeny, miny, moe	children's counting rhyme used when choosing something
recited	repeated from memory
wailing sound	high-pitched noise
ambulance	medical transport vehicle
wobbling	unsteady but not falling
precariously	dangerously, nearly falling
clambered	climbed
kerb	stone edge of a pavement
munching	chewing, eating
contemplating	thinking about
pressed her to her bosom	held her close
perch	rod or twig for a bird to sit on
creep up behind her	take her by surprise

Food for thought

1. Why did Annie's mother drop a baking tray?
    a. She was startled by a noise.
    b. She was angry with Annie for disturbing her.
    c. She was in a state of shock.

2. Which statement is true according to the story?
    a. Annie felt guilty about taking buns.
    b. Annie didn't take any buns until she was told she could have one.
    c. Annie ate all the buns.

3. Why didn't the ambulance wail when it drove off?
    a. There was no longer any need to use a siren.
    b. The ambulance was empty.
    c. The driver didn't want to frighten Annie.

4. Who or what was Joey?
    a. a playmate
    b. a toy
    c. a bird

5. Which word best describes Annie's state of mind at the end of the story?
    a. contented
    b. miserable
    c. concerned

Crossword puzzle

ACROSS

2 high-pitched noise
4 medical transport vehicle
9 repeated from memory
10 thinking about
11 inspected

DOWN

1 climbed
2 unsteady
3 chewing, eating
5 fuss
6 seat with no arms or back
7 a bird sits on this
8 upset, distressed

Picture quiz – medical emergencies

A The story involved a medical emergency. Below are some key medical words. Match them to the pictures.

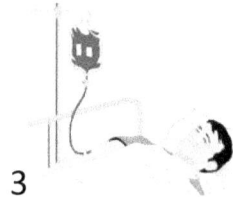

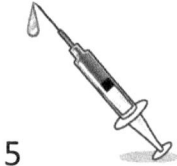

BLOOD PRESSURE MONITOR ( )   HYPODERMIC SYRINGE ( )
ANTI-CHOKING MANOEUVRE ( )   BLOOD TRANSFUSION ( )
CARDIOPULMONARY RESUSCITATION ( )   FIRST AID KIT ( )

B The picture below shows something mentioned in the story. Annie did not know what it is called. Unscramble the letters to find three different names for it.

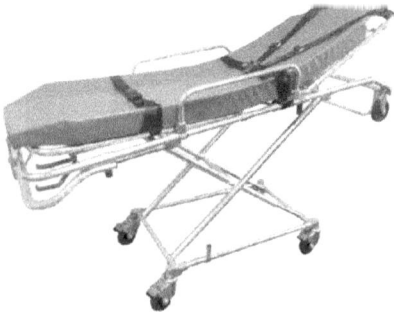

1 CHERTREST

2 YELLROT

3 YERUNG

Almost Persuaded

by Maurice Claypole

—⁊ ᪥ ᧚—

From deep behind the heavy door Patsy Cline was singing The Honky Tonk Merry Go Round accompanied by slide guitar and tinkling ivories. A brief hesitation, then warmth and light flooded momentarily into the street as the square-shouldered figure pushed open the door and entered. From inside, the voice wasn't quite Patsy Cline. Good, though, Hicks thought, as he heaved his weight onto a bar stool, nodding in the direction of the 'Bud on tap' sign and flipping a ten from his hip pocket onto the bar. After six days on the road his eyelids were heavy; it was as if he didn't see the hand that wiped the mahogany veneer with a cloth, placed a glass on a paper napkin and exchanged the ten for a five, a one, a quarter. As he took a gulp through the froth, he caught Doc Watson smiling at him from a faded signed photo behind the bar, a phony smile collecting dust in a tarnished frame. Above it a mirror revealed the singer, coal black hair cascading from a cowgirl hat, sequined jacket casting sparkles in his direction. She was into the next song and her eyes seemed to pick up his reflection as she sang, "Turn the cards slowly while you're dealing, darling." Swivelling on the stool, he cast his most fetching smile in her direction, neatly emulating the framed portrait. The way she moved brought back a box of memories: the hint of a ruby smile, the curve of a breast, slender fingers curling round a microphone. Now she was definitely looking in his direction. "So where do I go from here?" he wondered, pushing his empty glass across the bar. "Just don't let her know she's getting through to you, that's all. Life is just heartaches by the numbers, but who's counting?"

The song over, she stepped down, 'thank ye'all'- ing the less than appreciative audience, heading straight for the bar. An aspiring George Jones replaced her at the microphone and launched into a waltz: "Last night all alone in a ballroom ..."

She seemed to float across the floor, taking up a position on the stool next to Hicks. "Nice", she said, indicating the 'HH' on the breast pocket of his braided shirt. "Hickory Holler original," he replied, not taking his eyes off her. The vocals flowed over from the stage, "... and as she pressed her soft hand in mine, I found myself wanting to kiss her, for temptation was flowing like wine ..." More drinks appeared on the bar, the dwindling pile of bills being replaced by small change. The growing hubbub drowned their conversation, the no-longer new crystal chandeliers barely lighting up the paintings on the wall, the soft light adding an intimacy to the smoke-filled atmosphere of the bar room. Polite conversation turned into laughter, trembling lips formed into a genuine smile; a soft hand touched his, and as they left the bar for the cool darkness of the night, he placed an arm round her shoulders.

"The funny thing is," he sighed, as the saloon door closed behind them, "this time I didn't even get to Albuquerque."

"It makes no difference now," she smiled, hooking her arm in his, "Let's go home."

— ❧ ☙ —

Words and phrases

slide guitar	guitar playing technique sliding a steel or glass tube on one finger across the strings
tinkling ivories	sound of a piano being played gently (ivories = piano keys)
on the road	travelling
veneer	thin layer of wood used as a coating
napkin	small serviette
phony	fake, not genuine
tarnished	discoloured
cascading	falling in stages like a waterfall
sequined	covered with small shiny discs.
dealing	handing out playing cards in a game
swivelling	turning on the spot
fetching	charming
emulating	trying to copy or imitate
hint of	suggestion of, slight
less than appreciative	not expressing very much pleasure
aspiring	trying to become
braided	decorated with woven strips of cloth
dwindling	becoming smaller
hubbub	sound of a lot of voices
barely	only just, hardly

Food for thought

1. *'From inside, the voice wasn't quite Patsy Cline.'* What does this sentence tell us?
    a. The singer in the bar was trying to sing in the style of a famous singer.
    b. Hicks had expected to see Patsy Cline.
    c. What he could hear was a recording.

2. How was Hicks feeling when he ordered a drink?
    a. tired
    b. lonely
    c. disappointed

3. Why did Hicks swivel on his stool?
    a. Someone had called his name.
    b. He didn't want to see his reflection in the mirror.
    c. So that he could look directly at the singer.

4. How did the audience react when she finished her set?
    a. They applauded loudly.
    b. There wasn't much of a reaction.
    c. They expressed their displeasure.

5. What happens at the end of the story?
    a. The singer invites Hicks to her place.
    b. Hicks takes the singer to his trailer.
    c. We learn that Hicks and the singer are already a couple.

This story contains the titles of a number of Country & Western songs, as well as lines from different songs. You can understand the story without knowing the songs, but can you identify them? Search online for phrases from the story.

Word search

Find the words in the grid. Words can go horizontally, vertically or diagonally in any direction.

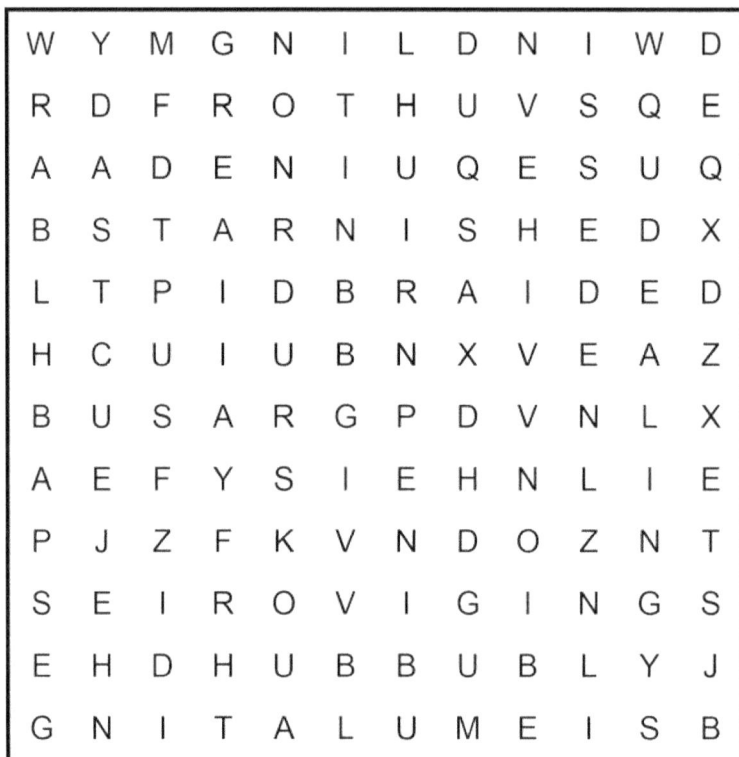

W	Y	M	G	N	I	L	D	N	I	W	D
R	D	F	R	O	T	H	U	V	S	Q	E
A	A	D	E	N	I	U	Q	E	S	U	Q
B	S	T	A	R	N	I	S	H	E	D	X
L	T	P	I	D	B	R	A	I	D	E	D
H	C	U	I	U	B	N	X	V	E	A	Z
B	U	S	A	R	G	P	D	V	N	L	X
A	E	F	Y	S	I	E	H	N	L	I	E
P	J	Z	F	K	V	N	D	O	Z	N	T
S	E	I	R	O	V	I	G	I	N	G	S
E	H	D	H	U	B	B	U	B	L	Y	J
G	N	I	T	A	L	U	M	E	I	S	B

aspiring
braided
dealing
dwindling

emulating
froth
hubbub
ivories

phony
sequined
slide guitar
tarnished

Picture quiz – money

A In the story, Hicks paid for his drinks in cash, but that isn't the only way to pay. Unscramble the money words below and match them to the pictures.

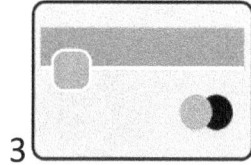

1   2   3

4   5   6

CLEANTCOSTS – ICON –
BINOCIT – CLASPIT – EFAS – KNOTBANE

Write the words below.

1 _____   2 _____   3 _____

4 _____   5 _____   6 _____

B Match the words below with the pictures. Answer by putting the numbers in the brackets.

1 combination ( )   **2** Chip & PIN ( )   **3** RFID ( )
4 quarter ( )   **5** paper ( )   **6** cryptocurrency ( )

Dotty

by Anthony Curtis

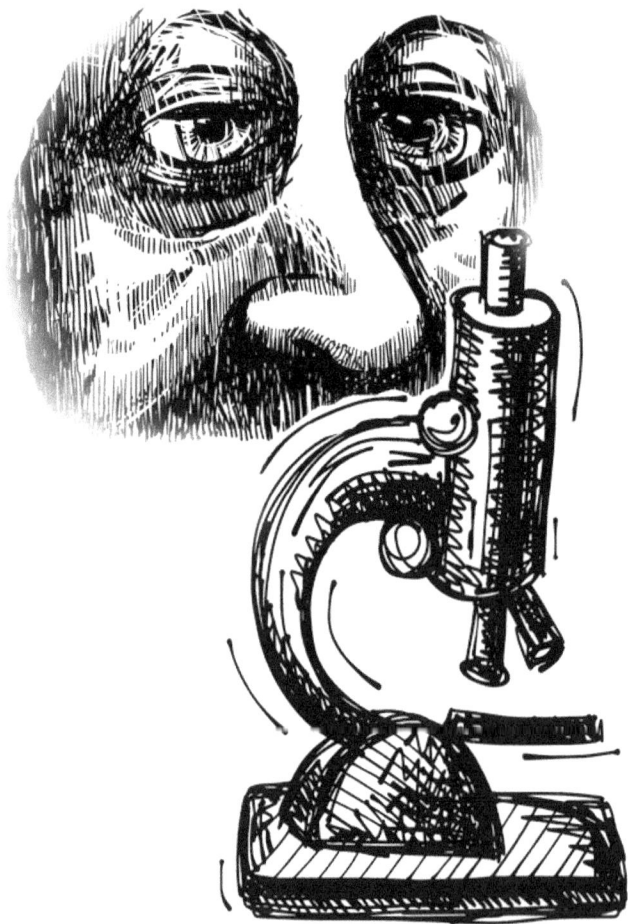

—— ❧ ❦ ——

Back in the 1950s, in a world before computers dominated people's lives, Professor Dunk was a lecturer in mathematics at a lesser-known university. He was known to his students as 'The Sparrow' due to his habit of cocking his head to one side when reading.

But Professor Dunk was more than just a mathematician. He secretly experimented with all kinds of things. One day he conducted an almost successful teleportation experiment. The theory, however, proved to be weaker than the practice, and his television set was teleported into another dimension, an event which caused the professor to decide that his findings should remain secret. After all, the world has enough problems as it is.

The professor was tempted to destroy the formula, but a page full of scribbled mathematical equations was, to him, equal to a Dürer or a Picasso. The formula was fifteen pages long, and as he was unable to store such a quantity of equations in his head, he gave them to a colleague, who promised to reduce them to microdots. He almost scratched his brains out trying of think of a suitable hiding place for the dots. Eventually he found one, and was confident that no one would ever find them. He purchased a powerful microscope and in the evenings would take the microdots from their hiding place, put them under the apparatus, and sit gazing into it. The image was slightly distorted, but that didn't bother him.

The theory he had published in the science journal 'New Inventions', however, attracted not only scientists, but also military experts, government departments and foreign spies, all of whom had the same goal: to get the formula at all costs.

Too eccentric to marry, Professor Dunk lived alone. He was never lonely though, for his interest in his studies transcended normality. Consequently, he was highly surprised when strangers began to show marked interest in him. Then came the alarming telephone calls. How could anyone dare to threaten the life of a little professor in a lesser-known university? People were after his formula!

Up to this time, no one had given the possibility of microdots a thought, for the professor didn't look like the microdot sort. However, the colleague who had shrunk the formula to almost nothing blabbed his heart out one evening to a platinum blonde who worked for the Defence Department. After ten glasses of whisky, he told her all about the microdots, but he had no idea where they were hidden.

Successfully enticing the professor out of his rooms with a seven-day free holiday in the Hebrides (it was the summer and everyone else was away), the Defence Department proceeded to examine every full stop, comma and dot in every book in the professor's rooms. After five days of intensive searching (nobody could hide something that well), they came to the conclusion that the professor has concocted a hoax and was on an ego trip. They were about to leave when one searcher happened to notice a microscope in the corner of the professor's room. Now what would a little professor of mathematics in a lesser-known university want with a large and expensive microscope? "Of course! Microdots have to be enlarged." The dots did exist.

"We'll find 'em," promised the Defence Minister, thankful that he didn't have to look.

"Ve vill get dem," asserted the foreign spies, "even if ve haf to blow ze old egg-head sky high."

"We'll brainwash him," said the CIA when Dunk had returned from the Hebrides, and they proceeded to do so.

"Where have you hidden the microdots?" demanded an exhausted interrogator.

"I'm wearing them," said the professor, lying spread-eagled on a bed.

"Where?" shouted the interrogator.

"Where? … Yes … wearing them," said the professor.

"Oh nuts. He isn't wearing a stitch. Shall we liquidate him?" asked the interrogator.

"Our methods may be devious," said the boss, "but we are not in the habit of liquidating little professors from lesser-known universities. Personally, I think he's just plain dotty. Take him home and put him to bed."

The microdots were never found.

Professor Dunk should have lived to a ripe old age, but in the middle of a new, 'improved' experiment, he managed to teleport himself into another dimension and was never seen again.

Where then, had the microdots been hidden?

The riddle was eventually solved by a cub reporter who had followed the professor like a relentless bloodhound. He was aware that the professor's students had nicknamed him 'the Sparrow' because of his head cocking habit, and he was also aware of the existence of the microscope. With a flash of genius he managed to persuade the professor's lawyers to show him a copy of the will, the ultimate phrase of which helped to satisfy his curiosity:

"… that upon my death I be cremated, wearing my contact lenses."

— ❧ ❦ —

Words and phrases

lesser-known	less famous
sparrow	common small bird
cocking his head to one side	turning the top of his head downwards and sideways
scribbled	written roughly by hand
scratched his brains out	thought very hard about
gazing	looking long and intently
at all costs	regardless of money or effort
eccentric	unconventional
transcended	was greater than
shrunk	made smaller
blabbed his heart out	revealed secret matters
enticing	tempting
isn't wearing a stitch	is naked
liquidate	kill
dotty	crazy, eccentric
ripe old age	very old age
riddle	puzzle, question
cub reporter	junior journalist
relentless bloodhound	steady pursuer, keen detective
will	testament
ultimate	last
cremated	burned to ashes

Food for thought

1. Why did the professor decide not to destroy the formula?
    a. Because he would never be able to write it again.
    b. He regarded it as a work of art.
    c. So that someone would find it one day.

2. Who let the cat out of the bag?
    a. Professor Dunk
    b. the professor's colleague
    c. a platinum blonde

3. When they saw the microscope, the members of the Defence Department
    a. realised that the story of the microdots was true.
    b. decided to send the professor away.
    c. knew they would have to liquidate the professor.

4. When the professor was interrogated...
    a. he lied to his tormentors.
    b. he went mad.
    c. he was wearing the microdots.

5. What finally happened to Professor Dunk?
    a. He was cremated.
    b. He lived a long time and died of natural causes.
    c. He vanished into thin air.

Word search puzzle

Solve the clues then find the answers in the grid.
Words can go horizontally, vertically or diagonally in
any direction.

burned to ashes	....
kill	....
last	....
made smaller	....
small bird	....
tempting	....
testament	....
unconventional	....
written roughly by hand	....

M	L	K	H	M	T	C	W	Z	C
R	I	X	V	Q	N	W	O	I	D
E	Q	S	N	N	W	T	R	M	E
N	U	C	H	I	H	T	R	X	T
T	I	R	L	R	N	R	A	T	A
I	D	L	Q	E	U	X	P	J	M
C	A	K	C	M	G	N	S	W	E
I	T	C	Y	L	F	D	K	P	R
N	E	T	A	M	I	T	L	U	C
G	S	C	R	I	B	B	L	E	D

Picture quiz – scientific instruments and ideas

A Label the instruments with words from the box.

1    2    3

4    5 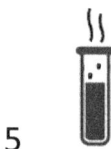   6

TEST TUBE	MICROSCOPE	FLASK
MAGNET	TELESCOPE	DIVIDERS

Write the words below.

1 _____   2 _____   3 _____

4 _____   5 _____   6 _____

B Unscramble the words under the images.

1    2    3 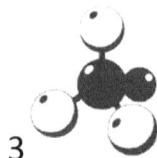   4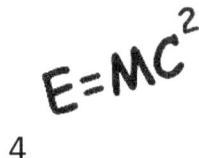

MOAT   AND   EMUOCELL   ROAMFUL

Coastal Encounter

by Shelly Bowers

— ৯ ৯ —

Every time I close my eyes and all I can see is a lonely old woman looking at me. The image of all my fears in life, she stands alone on the grey coastal road, alone in the wind and the rain, alone in her dreams and visions. I wish I had known her name, but now I don't even know if she was real. Yet I can still feel the pain of her story. It frightened me to see and touch the sorrow and loneliness that can cripple a mortal mind and shadow the human heart.

For myself, I had just broken off my long-term relationship with John and needing a holiday, I picked a cycling break around Ireland to help me 'discover myself', as the cliché goes. The weather had been dull all morning, threatening gales, so struggling to balance a bike and put on waterproofs, I tried to push ahead out of Cushendall. Walking along the road towards me was an elderly lady, heading into town. She smiled as we came to pass and I knew we were about to have a five minute conversation on the weather. It is an art perfected in Ireland. I tried to push the bike forward eager to reach the youth hostel, but I was too late and with a forced grin, I responded to an ambiguous comment about the miserable state of the sky. We stood together on the road and exchanged pleasantries on my holiday. Then, like a bolt from the blue, she changed the subject to ask me what kind of men I liked.

"You know, attracted to," she prompted.

I must have stood with my mouth open. This was a subject that I had rarely discussed with my mother without thinking of having a discussion with my grandmother, whom I judged to be a good ten years younger than this lady.

To me this scene had suddenly become so comical. My heart warmed to her youthful ways, as I stammered out that I was attracted to tall blond men.

"Ah! So you like the Scandinavian types with their big muscles," she laughed, nudging me in a conspiratorial manner, "I like dark swarthy men, with dark eyes which capture your soul."

Her voice became wistful against the wind and the waves.

"So it's an Italian you are after," I joked.

"No! No!" she said, "I like the men from the East, the desert places. You know, the Gulf and Kuwait."

The story she then told me was typical of any possessive teenage girl and I struggled to set it into the life that I imagined for her, of pension days, coupons and white hair rinses. Yet, as the story unfolded, I saw her become a woman in love as chaste as a June bride. She had met her Kuwaiti prince in the early days of spring, at Larne market. He was alone, grateful for the chatter, she had been willing to talk. Whenever she went to town on a Saturday, they would meet. The smile on her face grew as she told of their teas together and I wondered how they must have looked, his young dark sunny complexion in contrast to the small woman with white hair and weathered pale skin.

One afternoon, jokingly he had asked her to marry him, saying she was his only friend and he would whisk her away back to the Arabian land of Kuwait from miserable, wet Ireland.

I was suddenly jerked to attention – her voice was sincere, to her this was no jest. The love was real. She continued talking, lost in the tale, but her face had changed – a cloud of dark thought had invaded her world.

One Saturday he wasn't at the market, but she continued shopping, she visited the gift shops for some small token of love. Pain grew in her voice as she found words more difficult and her tale began to falter. I watched unable to interrupt as her hands rose in agitation continually forming fists. From what I could piece together, he hadn't noticed her enter the gift shop, engrossed as he talked with a young girlfriend. Blind with hurt and jealousy she marched between them. Raising her voice, she began to attack him for talking to another girl. Firstly shocked, he tried to talk her down, but she wouldn't let him speak, shouting him down with his own words. So, calmly he turned his back to her and guided the young girl from the shop, then he returned to her side and in a low, stinging voice asked how she dare embarrass him in front of his friends. Then turning abruptly, he left her abandoned. Her strained voice had dropped into silence, and tears welled up from her broken heart.

"Did you ever see him again?" I asked.

"Yes, many times, but he would just ignore me, crossing the street or taking off into the crowd." She reached her hand towards my face. "You look a lot like him."

I knew that my own dark short hair and brown skin had heightened her pain. We hadn't walked far when she asked me if she had been wrong. I was no longer to be the listener to the tale, I was being asked to participate, to offer some small token of comfort. Looking at her face and listening to her voice, I hesitated before telling her that I felt she had acted hastily in the shop, but he should have given her a chance to say sorry.

"Yes. Yes, he should have let me apologise. If he would let me say sorry, we could have a chance together."

She wanted so much to believe that there was hope. I became overwhelmed as I thought of lost friendships, plans and loves so deep and endlessly passionate.

"You hurt too."

As the feeling of loss flooded through my body the tears flowing faster, I nodded yes. Then almost naturally, we fell into each other's arms as the tears came. We shared the moment relying on each other for comfort, but there I lost her. Unable to deal with the pain she had brooded on for so long, she searched desperately for reassurance that her prince had not left her forever, that one day he would return. With a pleading look, she turned to me and asked, "When will he come back?"

For many years, I deliberated over my answer. Should I have told her he wouldn't be back? I thought I could help; I told her that he would return in the spring like the time she had first met him. I felt that I had given her a dream for a moment. A look of joy and hope came to light her face, this was all she had hoped for, a chance meeting to plan for.

The old spinster turned to me a final time and reaching out to touch my short dark hair she said, "I know he will come, because you are his messenger and you will ride off into the sky."

She pointed towards the horizon where a lone sunbeam played across the grey sea. Without an answer, she said goodbye and rounded the bend into town again.

Looking back, I query many things about this meeting. Did I create more mischief in her mind by giving her hope?

Most of all, I wonder if I had been a messenger for her, or she for me. For standing alone on the strand, I felt the heavy weight of being the loneliest person in the world and I knew then, as I turned around, I was starting the long journey back to John and love.

— ❧ ❧ —

Words and phrases

cripple	cause serious injury to, hurt badly
cliché	overused phrase or idea
gales	strong, stormy winds
eager	impatient, anxious
bolt from the blue	sudden surprise
attracted to	drawn towards
stammered out	said hesitantly with pauses
nudging	pushing gently
swarthy	dark-skinned
wistful	sad, melancholy
chaste	pure, virginal
whisk her away	take her quickly
no jest	serious, no joke
falter	become disconnected/hesitant
piece together	figure out, understand
engrossed	absorbed, fully occupied
token of comfort	sign of consolation
hastily	too quickly
overwhelmed	very emotional, upset
pleading	desperate, begging
mischief	trouble

Food for thought

1. How did the narrator react when she first saw the old woman?
   a. She was keen to be sociable and exchange pleasantries.
   b. She tried to avoid becoming engaged in a conversation.
   c. She stopped and waited for the old woman to speak.

2. *'I must have stood with my mouth open.'* This tells us that she was...
   a. astonished
   b. perplexed
   c. incredulous

3. The old woman tells a story of...
   a. a whirlwind romance.
   b. unrequited love.
   c. a shotgun wedding.

4. Why does the old woman call the narrator a messenger?
   a. Because she has been waiting for her to appear.
   b. Because they have both suffered for love.
   c. Because the narrator has given her hope.

5. At the end of the story, the narrator...
   a. is uncertain about the significance of meeting the old lady
   b. finds that all her problems have been solved.
   c. knows that she has helped someone.

Mystery word crossword puzzle

Complete the puzzle, except for the mystery words, then enter the letters from the box in the right order to find the solution.

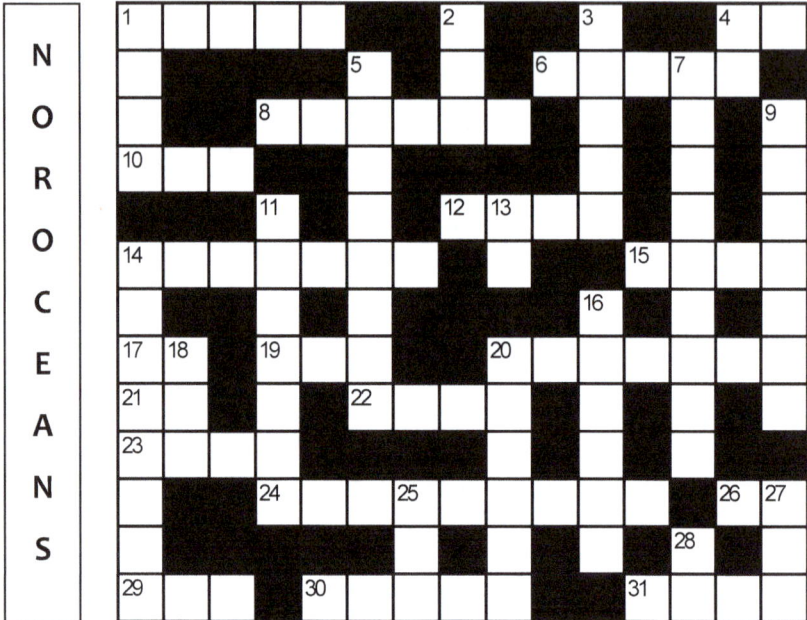

Letters box (left column): N O R O C E A N S

ACROSS

1 sign, gesture
4 you sit ... a bicycle to ride it
6 impatient, anxious
8 overused phrase
10 finish
12 what you no longer have
14 dark-skinned
15 injure, cause pain
17 impersonal pronoun
19 baked dish

20 MYSTERY WORD
21 negative answer
22 sea creature
23 spirit, inner being
24 absorbed
26 when, like or since
29 go very quickly on foot
30 push gently
31 joke

DOWN: Clues on next page

64

DOWN

1 story
2 what is left after burning
3 strong winds
4 either …
5 trouble
7 MYSTERY WORD
9 too quickly
11 hurt badly
13 preposition of belonging
14 unmarried woman
16 become hesitant
18 also
20 pure, virginal
25 colour of shame or anger
27 you can watch the sun … in the evening
28 exist

Picture quiz – describing people

Match the descriptions to the pictures.

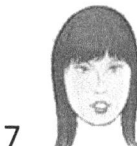

1 2 3 4

5 6 7 8

1 He's dark skinned with a little beard.
2 She has long straight hair and a fringe.
3 She wears her hair up in a bun.
4 He's fair-haired with a quiff.
5 He's clean shaven and fairly swarthy.
6 She's got pigtails.
7 She wears glasses and brushes her hair to one side.
8 He's thin on top and wears glasses.

Answer key

Lost Dreams

Food for thought
1 c **2** a **3** b **4** c **5** a

Crossword puzzle

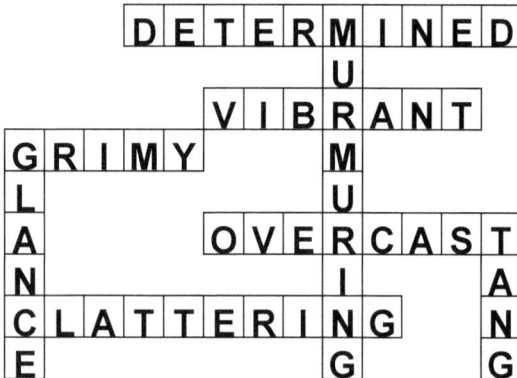

```
      D E T E R M I N E D
            U
        V I B R A N T
G R I M Y   M
L           U
A       O V E R C A S T
N           I       A
C L A T T E R I N G   N
E           G       G
```

Picture quiz

A
1 TANKARD   **2** DARTBOARD   **3** BAR STOOL   **4** ICE BUCKET
5 BEER BARREL   **6** BEER MUG

B
1 (5)   **2** (6)   **3** (2)   **4** (3)   **5** (1)   **6** (4)

Annie

Food for thought

1 c **2** b **3** a **4** c **5** a

Crossword puzzle

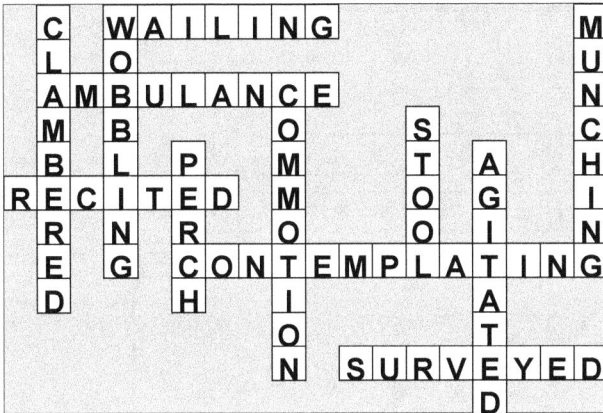

```
C  W  A  I  L  I  N  G                    M
L  O                                      U
A  M  B  U  L  A  N  C  E                  N
M  B        O        S              A      C
B  L     P  M        T              G      H
R  E  C  I  T  E  D  M              I      I
R  N     R  O        O              T      N
E  G     C  O  N  T  E  M  P  L  A  T  I  N  G
D        H  I                       A
            O     S  U  R  V  E  Y  E  D
            N                       T
                                    D
```

Picture quiz

A

BLOOD PRESSURE MONITOR (6)   HYPODERMIC SYRINGE (5)

ANTI-CHOKING MANOEUVRE (2)   BLOOD TRANSFUSION (3)

CARDIOPULMONARY RESUSCITATION (4)   FIRST AID KIT (1)

B

1 STRETCHER **2** TROLLEY **3** GURNEY

Almost Persuaded

Food for thought
1 a **2** a **3** c **4** b **5** c

Word search

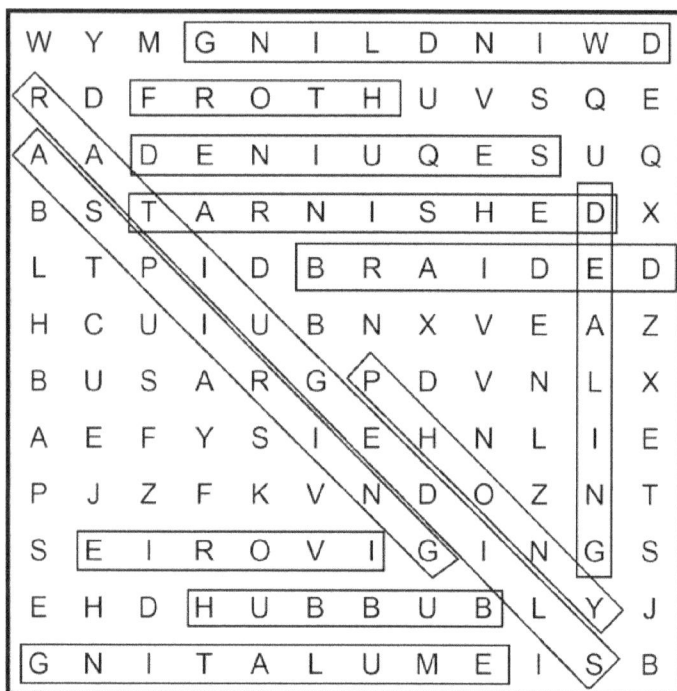

Picture quiz
A
1 COIN **2** BANKNOTE **3** PLASTIC
4 SAFE **5** BITCOIN **6** CONTACTLESS

B
1 (4) **2** (3) **3** (6) **4** (1) **5** (2) **6** (5)

Dotty

Food for thought
1 b   **2** b   **3** a   **4** c   **5** c

Word search puzzle

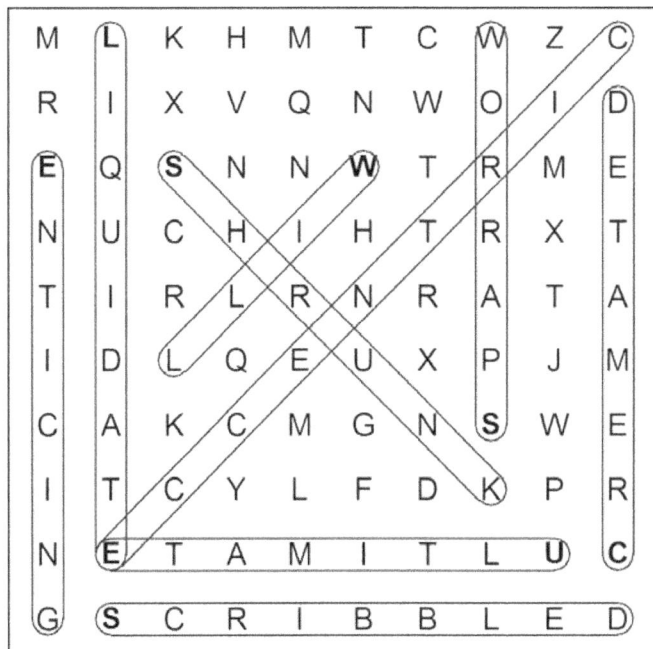

Picture quiz
A
1 TELESCOPE   **2** DIVIDERS   **3** FLASK
4 MAGNET   **5** TEST TUBE   **4** MICROSCOPE

B
1 ATOM   **2** DNA   **3** MOLECULE   **4** FORMULA

Coastal Encounter

Food for thought
1 b   **2** a   **3** b   **4** c   **5** a

Mystery word crossword puzzle

T	O	K	E	N			A			G			O	N
A					M		S		E	A	G	E	R	
L			C	L	I	C	H	E		L		N		H
E	N	D			S					E		C		A
			C		C		L	O	S	S		O		S
S	W	A	R	T	H	Y		A			H	U	R	T
P			I		I					F		N		I
I	T		P	I	E			C	O	A	S	T	A	L
N	O		P		F	I	S	H		L		E		Y
S	O	U	L					A		T		R		
T			E	N	G	R	O	S	S	E	D		A	S
E					E		T		R		B		E
R	U	N		N	U	D	G	E			J	E	S	T

Solution: C O A S T A L   E N C O U N T E R

Picture quiz

1 (8)   **2** (7)   **3** (4)   **4** (6)   **5** (1)   **6** (5)   **7** (2)   **8** (3)

Further titles from LinguaBooks

IN A STRANGE LAND
Short Stories for Creative Learning
Andrzej Cirocki and Alicia Peña Calvo   ISBN 978-3734789465

IN A STRANGE LAND is a collection of four original short stories which provide teachers with motivating and engaging classroom material at the CEFR B2 to C1 level and young adult learners with thought-provoking narratives and characters to whom they can relate.

This gripping teenage fiction encourages readers to use their imagination and interact with the texts in a variety of educational and experimental ways.

The stories are supported by creative tasks which enable students to integrate their various language skills, exploit computer technology, practise learning strategies and exercise autonomy.

Audio recordings of the stories are available on two separate CDs which are suitable for classroom use and can also be listened to for pleasure.

Academic Presenting and Presentations
A preparation course for university students
Peter Levrai and Averil Bolster   ISBN 978-3734783678

This practical training course is designed to help students cultivate academic presentation skills and deal with the variety of presentation tasks they may need to master during their studies.

The material is suitable for a global audience and can be used in a wide range of academic contexts since the content not only helps learners develop their presentation skills in English but also considers wider topics relevant to English for Academic Purposes, such as principles of research and the risk of plagiarism.

The accompanying online video presentations enable learners to immerse themselves still further in the material presented and witness first-hand the impact of the techniques illustrated.

A separate Teacher's Book is also available: ISBN: 978-3741242090

Developing Learner Autonomy Through Tasks
Theory, Research, Practice

Andrzej Cirocki   ISBN 978-1-911369-01-1

At the heart of this study is the fostering of learner autonomy in the language classroom, in particular how learner autonomy can be developed through pedagogical tasks. The work focuses on four different approaches: learner-related, classroom-related, resource-related and technology-related.

Developing Learner Autonomy through Tasks combines classroom theory, research and practice, all of which are immersed in the philosophy of social constructivism, whereby knowledge and learning are seen as both the context for and the result of human interaction.

"This is the book everyone in the field has been waiting for. It is the product of excellent classroom research... highly engaging, relevant, readable, and above all, practical in its handling of the issues."
- Prof. John McRae, University of Nottingham, UK

Controversies in ELT
What you always wanted to know about teaching English
but were afraid to ask
Maurice Claypole   ISBN 978-1-911369-00-4

This thought-provoking and informative collection of essays covers a broad spectrum of topics relating to English language teaching, including chapters on The Death Of the Communicative Approach, Teaching the Language of Sex and Teaching English in Second Life.

Also released for the first time in book form are chapters on the author's unique insight into the correlation between language, set theory and fractal mathematics - and the consequences for English teachers.

"This book provides a refreshing look at old concepts, opens our eyes to new perspectives and encourages teachers to venture along new paths."
- Elke Schulth, ELTAS, Germany

"Interesting... instructive and - not least - fun to read. A brilliant book!"
- Nick Michelioudakis, TESOL Greece

www.ingramcontent.com/pod-product-compliance
Lightning Source LLC
LaVergne TN
LVHW051709080426
835511LV00017B/2817